Sharon Chmielarz
DIFFERENT ARRANGEMENTS

CROW APPLEBLOSSOMS

Sharon Chmielarz

DIFFERENT ARRANGEMENTS

with drawings by Gaylord Schanilec

Minnesota Voices Project #10

New Rivers Press 1982

Typesetting: Peregrine Coldtype
Book design: C. W. Truesdale
Key-lining: Daren Sinsheimer
Editor for this book: Roger K. Blakely

The author wishes to thank the editors of the following magazines for permission to reprint some of the poems in this book: *English Journal* ("The Writing Lesson"); *Full Circle* ("The Sweeper"); *Great River Review* ("For Carl"); *Lake Street Review* ("Rock Climbing on the North Shore"); *Loonfeather* ("Crows," "A Rock near Lutsen," "The Shower," and "The Red Horse"); *Milkweed Chronicle* ("Old Lines" and "The Woman who Haunts the Jokaki Inn"); *Minnesota Monthly* ("Lines"); *North Country Anvil* ("Young Birch"); *Quindaro* ("A Reflection: On Relief"); *Passages North* ("My Father and Mother"); *St. Benedict's College Literary Magazine* ("Carl's Stone"); *Sing, Heavenly Muse* ("Having Tea on a Rainy Afternoon" and "Near the Iris"); and *Storystone* ("Ice Cream Panache").

New Rivers Press wishes to thank the following organizations and agencies for their generous support of THE MINNESOTA VOICES PROJECT: The Jerome Foundation, the Metropolitain Regional Arts Council, the Northwest Area Foundation, and the United Arts Fund.

New Rivers Press books are distributed by:
Small Press Distribution, Inc.   Bookslinger
1784 Shattuck Avenue   330 East 9th Street
Berkeley, CA 94709   St. Paul, MN 55101

DIFFERENT ARRANGEMENTS has been manufactured in the United States of America for New Rivers Press, Inc. (C. W. Truesdale, editor/publisher) 1602 Selby Ave., St. Paul, MN 55104 in a first edition of 1000 copies.

For all my Teachers,
and Tad

Different Arrangements

Catching Myself On Thin Air

TRELLIS AND IRISES

In the Living Room

In the living room
my father sits alone.
He's crying.
He doesn't know
I'm there.
The amazement is all mine,
watching how his chair
gets bigger and bigger,
how the room slowly runs
into a box,
how my legs are reduced
to saltwater
and I slip
back outside,
catching myself
on thin air.

Ice Cream Panache

Hot summer night.
We sit in the dark.
My mother with her bowl
and me with the other ½ pint.
It tastes good
but not sweet enough.

We don't talk.
We have a spoon in our mouth.
We use one hand to hold the bowl,
the other to wave the spoon
as we lick it off—
ice cream panache.

One thing's wrong.
The spoons keep ticking on the bowl.
If a Sisyphean mound appeared
we'd gladly volunteer
to eat it up
if it would block the door

for what sooner or later
will appear with father's
icy silence. Substitute ice
for fire and cream for love:
ice cream panache. It tastes
good, but not sweet enough.

Friday Night at the Showhall

On Fridays
when he takes us to the
movies, I sit between my
dad and my mom.

They do their duty,
keep the bad men
out of the cliffs around me.
It's my imagination

that sees one,
crouched in dad's shoulder,
gun aimed at my mother,
ready to open fire.

On the Kitchen Floor

It has blue lineoleum with swirls
like waves. Yellow from the wax.
Ma's waxing it some-more. I want
to pound her butt: Tell me why Dad's
mean! "Don't walk on the floor."

Now I'm at the table, wiggling
on the highstool. I make one leg
fall into the waves—ker-plunk!
Then he throws his kool-aid in her face.
I don't want to eat anymore.

I slide off the stool.
Under the tabletop is a treetrunk
with two big roots where I sit.
My dad's workshoes go by.
He's going out to the garden.

The floor is rumbling. It's
thundering...now it's sunny again.
This is my house. The tablecloth
is my curtain. I'm the only one here
who can hide on the floor.

Near the Iris

Imagine you're the five-year old,
standing beside the bed of iris,
dressed in your mom's old raincoat.
from inside the house
comes the sound of a piano
gone wild: your father
is pounding away on your mother,
a sound punctuated by soft
protestations, an occasional
scream after the thud of a
perfectly-placed hit.

This sound you know is all
out of musical balance.
You concentrate on the beautiful
fists of the iris,
their softness.

You try to stay away
from the edge of your stomach.
Which way to go?

this is a problem a lost
love-ring must have. The sound
you hear keeps looking for it—
the wrong place fingered
over and over.

It's here,
near the iris,
misplaced in mom's raincoat
pocket. It's there,
in the house, inside father's
infallible fist.

Dead Heat

It's hot in the kitchen.
Ma dumps the wash on the table.

I try to figure out if she did it,
what my dad beats her for.

And whether she'll go to hell.

Her head nods as she sprinkles.

She lays out his white Sunday shirt.
It takes up all the table, a preacher
waving his arms. She sprinkles it,

crosses the sleeves over the middle,
rolls it, stacks it, waits
until the iron is good and hot.

Tables

I remember the first table
had a chipped enameled top and a thin
lip of a drawer for silverware.
The legs were German: they insisted
on standing straight
on a rolling lineoleum floor.
Once—after he chased her
round and round the table, grabbing
for hair to hold her down as he
pounded—Olson's furniture van drove up
and delivered a new table.

Go ahead, Olson said, try it out.
There's more room to stretch your feet.
You can uncross your ankles.
There's more elbow room,
more space to set the dishes.
What's the matter, don't you like it?

The edge of this table
sticks in my guts.

Way Out of the Yard

Here is the yard
cut into halves
by the sidewalk Dad laid
two bricks wide.
It leads around the house
to the picket fence
which splits the yard into quarters.
In the middle is the trellis,
the heart of the yard,
the hole in the wall
Dad's fist made
when he couldn't get through
the yard
he fenced in, tied up and
wrapped like a present.

I'm inside.
If I step on a crack
my mom gets whacked.
I slip under the trellis,
past the iris to the lilacs.
Pick a leaf—a ticket
to Paris on the swing.
I'm off the ground,
way out of the yard,
out of the present.

In Paris, With Gertrude Stein

TEACUP AND ROSES

In Conversation with Gertrude Stein

What I read into the sentence
is my fantasy:
I'm watching Alice B. Toklas
serve *Eiskaffee* for tea.

She holds the tray
for Gertrude Stein,
Fernande Olivier,
and last, for me.

Fernande's titters
as she glances at my ankles
close together make me wonder
who she is.

Gertrude Stein intercepts
the thought, explains
how Fernande is close
to Picasso and moves on
to talk of cars. Fords.

Don't ever, she advises
learn reverse.
Just get the stick
out of diddle and dawdle
and slip into third.

I don't like the lurch
says Alice as Fernande
licks whipped cream
from the corners of her lips.

I take another cookie—
they're superb, but crumbly.
I brush off my chest. Crumbs
fly all over the page.

Alice fades, looking spotty.
I have to leave, a little early.
And the other two agree,
yes, I really must go home.

Alice B. Toklas Talks to Gertrude Stein

Tonight your shadow falls
as real in the room as the air
coming through the windows, carrying
the flavor of the street below—
footsteps in the midnight rain,
strong calls of old women
selling flowers to lovers—
violets to be kissed
on a lover's breasts.

For your desk, these yellow roses,
my arrangement for you to come to me:
for I've seen you lately, Gertrude Stein,
at salons, sitting quietly in your last
success: you've reversed
death's order by your presence.
Though you listen now more than you ask
or perhaps ask by listening—
I'm learning, Gertrude Stein!

I practice getting questions
back into their landscapes.
I open blocks of words, limn
answers along contoured lines.
And when I can no longer think
I go to your desk to touch
one petal of my quiet, yellow rose.
Come, my genius! Draw again a rose
in the black print of my words.

At the Banquet to Honor Rousseau

Apollinaire was to be there!
And I wanted badly to be there and
I came, too, on Gertrude Stein's
long sentences and sat near the door
though not so far back as some poor
woman who waited all night alone
in the courtyard for her man.
Fernande fixed the *ríz* and Salmon
(who obviously had a drinking problem)
jigged on top the saw-horse tables.
When he ate the brilliant yellow *fantaisie*
off Alice's new black velvet hat
Gertrude Stein came over,
asked me where I was from in Dakota.
"Near the Standing Rock Sioux Reservation."

Suddenly the center moved toward me.
Apollinaire asked me to sing 'red airs.'
My fingers drumming on the planks, I
droned what I'd heard in the westerns
and they liked it and
Miss Stein was glad I had something
americaine to offer and
if they all saw through it,
so? It was fun! It was 'rigolo.'
Then Apollinaire jumped up to sing his poem.
We all sang response,
"La peinture de ce Rousseau"
and it was great and I felt French,
Gertrude Stein, and thanks
for letting me come in on your long sentences.

A Case of Credentials

From my window I watched the girl leave,
flirting with a boyfriend. When the hall
was clear, I slipped inside her room,
lifted the box-lid, brushed aside the note
to the "shameless thief in this pension"
and took her invitation to the salon...

which I'm handing Miss Stein now,
along with my professor's recommendation...

oh, yes, I badgered him for it.
I hounded him. Studying with Gertrude Stein
would change the direction of my life.
I made him learn my face from his other
hundred students. He finally wrote
of my outstanding achievement, general
recognition and the tenacity of my habits...

At last, I'm in her study,
surrounded by masterpieces,
at the turning point in my life! The end
of her nose dips when she talks.
How could she let herself get so fat?
Do she and Miss Toklas really make love?
What is love like?

Why I Never Made it to #7 Rue de Fleurus

In the rue Laffitte
is the confectioner Fouquet.
Who could pass by his window
without buying one honeycake?
Not Gertrude Stein. Not I.

We talked of difference,
the delicacy of the honeycake
to the apple pie:
fruit sliced savagely,
dumped into a thick, sugary crust
and boiled in its own juice until done.
So American, so wonderful
in its own violent way.

She lived in # 7 rue de Fleurus.
Did I care to call? then bring
a friend, tonight, and she was gone
through Fouquet's tinkling doorway.

A friend? the Italian?
He helped me find the room-key,
calmed the concierge,
asked me, why, what was wrong
to sit upon my bed and

NO!
I'd rather sit in my room alone
than go to Gertrude Stein's with him!
—*S'il vous plâit*, I'll take
two dozen honey cakes instead.

At Gertrude Stein's Country House

I don't like Alice.
Somedays she's content
to be mistress,
and somedays behind closed doors
she's mean-voiced to Gertrude Stein.

But you can talk to Alice
about green grocers, perfumes,
five-minute cooking and tomatoes—
how she appreciated by Big Boys,
each over three pounds!

And I understand
why she chides Gertrude Stein—
a genius—
spending all her free time
romping with those dogs,
Basket and Pépé.

I've seen her come in for tea,
her bodice matted with dog hair.
Without washing her hands she takes
a cake directly from the plate and
feeds it to Pépé, her *baby*

talking more to it, if you please,
than she talks to us.

Lines

SUNFLOWERS AND MUSICAL RAIN

Old Lines

Still in the bird lie all the lines
to snake. The tail shorter, the fangs
sharpen to beak. In the same way
their small heads cock, their bodies start
at the noise of a leaf.

The same onyx eyes in the snake
I see in the sparrow perched on a rail
in the sun. Feathers and random streaks
congeal to scaled skin with stripes flowing
evenly, classically down the clean back

into the belly and rising in patterns
as highly structured as Alhambra's mosaics.
Picture a snake there.
It writhes its *s* across the patterned tiles
sensing ahead on the mosque's porch

near an arch a great deluge of sun.
Hard to decide which pattern—
the tiles' or the scales' or the snake's—
offers the most careful surprise.
Ancient snake. Ancient struggle,

when the ancestor still lives.
It strips down to a raw hunger
for each other. You've seen the bird's talons
drip with dead snake, or the snake force
slowly down its long tube neck, the bird.

Low warning rattles, quick snaps in the grass.
Nervous rhythms of ingestion. Then come
the liquid movements, the bird's song,
and from the snake's dark dwelling
its practiced silence, perfect sound.

Picture of Grandmother

This shot's blurred
as her name—Granma—
a title, a vague line
between the gray shape·
resting in the shade, and me.

And the head is my Uncle Henry's
who was sitting beside her,
last of five children, a mongoloid.
He was flapping his hands and
acting as if he were talking.

He's the boy in her story:
how he got boiling water
spilled on him when he was born.
Since then
they've never been alone.

She sits still
as a rabbit
whose heart
waits
in its throat.

"Smile," I say, trying
to focus the camera
on Granma,
blocking Henry
out of my picture.

She presses her lips
the camera clicks just as
the lines blurr—
Uncle Henry moved,
closer to her.

Sweetbread

I sometimes think of grandmothers
and grandfathers when they were young—
in the kitchen in the winter. Outside
the snow fence, stiff in the sugar snow.

Roused by the smells in the kitchen—
raisins, yeast and a bosom's oil—
they turned to each other. And when they returned,
they spent the rest of the day making things.

Remembering her breasts and thighs
and the horses he harnessed each day,
he carved shyly, hinting.
Some of these thoughts must be true—

the clock, his chair, I am here
in the kitchen, writing. What is it like
to work with a file after a summer of
handling the plow? I pretend.

Bending over the paper, I press my pen with
knuckled concentration. Round each vowel.
Speak each consonant as it's being written.
Make the black lines straight. The lines
fence in white banks. I've spent the afternoon

stomping through snow, arriving at *Oma*'s and *Opa*'s
too early—the dough not yet risen, not even set,
too early for *Oma* to give me sweetbread to eat.

On Hearing of his Brother's Death

letter from England
to Minnesota, Dec. 1981

On hearing of his brother's death
Uncle Czeslaw, 80, writes to us
in shaky script. The "y" in his 'sorry'
grows out of the rubble, a weed
in a row of devastated words.

"Things are very bad," he writes,
"I have lost my only brother
and my sister in Poland is upset.
We had 5 sisters and 3 brothers
and only 2 are left.

"I am sending parcels to Poland,
food and clothing
for the grandchildren.

"My sister lost her husband this year.
My sister's son lost his wife this year.

"I was talking to my brother.
In Warsaw. In 1938.
And I have not seen him since."

The Shower

An evening shower
passes over
the brown pond.

In the water
raindrops, reeds,
and a skiff's shadow

waver—
Over an unrolled parchment,
old music.

Lines

for H.G.J.

The lines of a skiff
   simple, swift, direct
reflected in the water
   near a dock
on a shore in the woods.

Nothing lovelier
than patience,
buoyancy of purpose: to stay afloat
quietly. To cross the water
by keel.

Forget the water
is in the Moreau or the Molstead.
It's *like*
the ocean's. And in part,
it is.

The Hook

The way it hangs there
the tail of my "g"
looks like a fish hook,
so sharp
I'd hate to run into it.
It's bad enough, making it,
taking those kind of orders
from my fingers.
Imagine the brain
directing them!

There, there!
I may only be fishing,
trying to hook something
from the waves below,
that great, vast, watery
I-don't-know.

Copy for an Ad

Give your mother a box of Richman's
chocolate-covered sugar-strychnine.
Make the old bag retch. Get back at her
for not living up to her potential,
for putting you through college,
writing letters that hinted
she was tired.
Get back at her for having big feet,
piano legs, round shoulders
and big boobs,
for passing them all onto you,
except for the boobs.
Get back at that she-goat
for swearing on the Bible
you didn't have big feet
and for the other compliments
she made up.
Now that she's fat and liver-spotted
and can't run away,
give her candy. Enough to eat
until her guts hang out.
Give her two, *three*
boxes of Richman's samplers,
in the name of mother, daughter,
profiteer.

Angel's House

for AE – d. 1977

Beside the tracks and railroad roundhouse
Angel's house in South Dakota looks like Zhivago's
weathered *dacha*. Or a lumberyard

with stacks of boards along the walk
to the back door and in the basement—
a firetrap, three inches deep in sawdust.

(Angel built the house for Mary
when he first came to this country.
He's sober now but she never came back.)

In the middle of the cellar's gloom
Angel stands, pushing the heart of the pine
board through the blade of the saw.

It's almost One. He snaps the saw's
whine off. Sawdust settles on Angel's
cap, shoulders, dark-blue sleeves.

The room is full of quiet
hills of handmade chairs and stars
pieced together and inlaid on tables.

Angel shuffles to a shelf,
turns on the radio and lies down
on the bench near the furnace.

Hands behind his head, he rests
his wild Bulgarian-brown eye while
from under thick eyebrows the milky one

stares off and makes you wonder
if Angel's looking here or there.
Now it's One and

from Carnegie Hall Milton Cross
announces to his radio audience
in South Dakota the NBC Texaco opera—

Angel's kind of music,
like woodburn and a saw's edge it has
the pitch he heard first in Bulgarian.

For Carl

And if you were invited into Carl's kitchen,
you'd like the corners, stuffed with relics—
a wooden hat rack that sags with papers,
the wooden rocker of dead Uncle Henry,
a milk separator and the farm-white cupboard.
From out the kitchen window
you'd look into the windbreak pines.

Winters in this rattling kitchen
Carl writes on picture cards—
purple ponies and bison-skin tipis.
He recalls summer evenings.
He stands in the wheat fields,
he can smell the harvest
coming up on the wind
from miles and miles to the south,.
He dreams of the past,
of his three younger brothers,
of Sioux points and hammers
and flint-headed hide scrapers
he's plowed up in potato and cornfields.
He tends his arrowheads.
He gives some away.

You can see the rest,
lying in the county museum,
neat under a block of glass,
for Carl has joined the others in the windbreak pines
who plow the earth with horses each morning
        when there's haze,
who walk the hot dirt farm roads on restless afternoons
and dance at night with tall sunflowers to the moaning wind
sweetly full of cornflower, flax and wheat.
Whispering like the pines

they spirit his old frame farmhouse,
tease the dreamers sleeping hot on top Carl's bed.
And when the wind plays tricks
by banging doors or lids,
they all laugh loudly as the bodies jerk
and crack their spirit dance.
And all this is right, for Carl.

A Reflection: On Relief

When people are poor then all should share
in the surplus the government sent,
the apples, the hams. We never saw none.
Tramps ate better than us
on what I bought with a dollar a day
when I had it. One day we woke up,
your mother and I, two babies
and no food in the house.
When I asked for work they laughed, "Ted,
you don't need a job." So I begged.
The preacher was there, looking for work;
he got it and kept it for himself.

Winter of '36 I found work on the tracks.
Though I piled on clothes I froze
stiff as the bread I ate.
That summer I dug ditches;
once near the tent where the town
fed tramps when they came off the tracks.
A tramp from New York watched
me eat my bread. "Eat with us today,"
he said. Even on the farm,
I never tasted better ham.

There was talk about a cellar
near the roundhouse, full of surplus.
I was the only one who'd go in.
"Hey, where do you think you're going?"
yelled the pipsqueak near the stairs.
"Hey, where do you think you're going?"
yelled his boss.
Downstairs from the ceiling on hooks
hung the hams, waiting for distribution.
A few went to the tramps,

the rest when to the people
who could buy them.

Rich bastards in town
had got a hold of our surplus,
people with connection,
friends of the priest—
so they gave some hams away—
to people like the woman
who stood right here and told me
since I had a home—a two-room shack—
I didn't need no help.
If she'd been a man
she'd be laying flat.
And me and your mother
went hungry. And our children.

And not the only ones,
Ted said to get himself quieted down,
and not the only ones.

With The Thunder, Tea

TEACUP AND POPPIES

Having Tea on a Rainy Afternoon

You can feel the rain in your hips now.
With the thunder, tea—foreign
out here. Take it at your window,
look out to your garden's
thimbleweed, wild prairie onion,

farther on, some hidden rose.
Back to Odessa. A ring in your ear,
the stifling room, the samovar

you serve. Flight. In an antiquarium
for days you roam, handling the dark
maroon black bindings, trying to get
through the books' black print and musk,

At the end of long rows of books,
on some unseen cornershelf, a wireless,
dust-covered, plays all day softly,
concerti written only for one violin

High Tea

Three women step out of the loggia
to whiteglove the garden statue.
They bend observations on the flowers
between teacups and white lives.
Their conversation is a proscenium:
"Her marriage, so exciting!"
"For her mother, terrifying."

Cups click on a silver tray.
It's time to go home to their men.
One woman's last words
like the linden's leaves
shadow the stonewall around them:
"I'm glad Mama died when I was young."

The Uniform

On the garden walk
I look like all the others—
middle-aged women in suits,
ooing and ahing to flowers—

though something's missing—
the memory of pink muslin,
a dress with small brass buttons
his quick fingers opened—

An equivalent for Eros—
a love of gardens, madras, lilacs—
fills the gap—
his handspace to our hearts.

Erika at her Table

for Erika:
"Ich korrespondiere
mit der ganzen Welt."

Little finger raised,
Erika sips from her cup.

She writes "to the whole world,"
other refugees.

She eats boiled potato
mashed in cottage cheese

on an ice-cube tray
her husband Josef found.

Her dreams
are of Caspian gardens,

trim uniforms
worn by St. Petersburg girls.

She remembers Papa,
the Duke's own brewer,

and Mama,
whose last name meant noble.

That's where the dreams
stumble into her table—

the noble slips
into a cup of war and lines

of displaced persons.
What could have been, turns

to the texture of tea.
See it, in her watery eyes.

Old Woman in Wabasha, MN

Beside her porch,
one push away from falling in,
the old woman sits
under a blossoming plum.
Like her, already
fizzled out at the end of spring.

She gets her tools and
goes out to the garden.
Fork and hoe—
they're her horses now
and she's the plow—
lurch down one weedy row
and stop.

She waits
for her body to settle down, then
her lean-shouldered companions
take her back home.

The Woman who Haunts the Jokaki Inn

She was confused by the loose
abandonment she felt in death.
It came too soon
after her parents'
and the ride into the desert
to stay with the Sisters.
She got sick and lay
in the school's infirmary
in a row of empty cots.
No place could be more quiet.
She wished for death
and got it.

                    She's watched
the casket with her body
carried easily across the courtyard
and buried near the church.
She's watched the school
change hands and become
an inn. She remains
out of touch with time.

She looks in the lobby's window.
No shadow or reflection in the glass
persuades her to stay.
She looks from guest to guest
for a glance of permission
to enter the present—
like schoolgirls, we keep
our eyes politely averted.

Stranglehold

The woman—
near the oriental poppies—
has 14 arms
around a kicking
child.

A whisper
slides through her teeth.
"Be quiet!
And we'll go see
the pond."
Mother and daughter

stand together
and break the glass
surface with fistfuls
of rocks.

Hannah's Horn

Based on I Samuel 1, 2:1-10

Hannah's womb
had been shut by the Lord.
It was not enough
that Elkanah loved her more than ten sons
or more than Penninah, his other wife,
and all her children.

In the House of the Lord
at a post near a pillar
Hannah wailed to the Lord
like a drunken handmaid
or a bargaining shrew.

Back at home she trimmed the wicks,
filled the bins—the cask of flour
puffed when opened. On the shelf
the cruets shone with wine and honey.
At the well the women teased
and patted her growing belly.

After the birth, Hannah loved awakening,
moving through the dark in the room
to suckle her son. At his name, Samuel,
all rigidity melted into order.
Her single obsession flowed like a river

and she sang:
God is Rock. He has set
the world on pillars.
Forever will the barren
sing praises to His power.
He has opened my womb,
calling "Samuel"—
the voice that answers,
"Here am I", is half-mine.

Reminiscing

for Ella Grace Clara

Something about the swallows
circling overhead
reminds her of a story.
She goes back sixty years
to swallows circling above a quarry.
Two girls are playing hide-and-seek.
Mom's the younger girl, cutting through
her dad's wheatfield to the quarry
where she finds her friend
hiding near the ledge
where swallows build mud nests.

"Cup your hands for a secret."
She cups them and the secret
shits into her palm.

What is it she remembers most?
the shrieks of fun? rubbing shit hard
into her friend's chest? the surprise
of finding breasts, rising, beating
like a scared bird's wings?
Their laughter hesitates
then fades in echoes through the quarry.

One-Night Stands

CROW APPLEBLOSSOMS

Rock Climbing on the North Shore

for Vicki J.

From the shambles of her rage,
the mind throwing itself to the ground,
kicking, screaming, "I can't, you won't,"

the eye of silence

watches the sun's disciplined
climb up the rock, notices
a ledge of harebells, the first foothold,

motion the body to a forward response.

Slow to find stirrups.
Slowly she opens the stock
of her body. Here is the body,

here the calm rock

here the rock winds.
Under her crotch, a broad leather palm.
Under her boot, crumbling shale.

How patient the movement of the rock
in descent as the apprentice ascends,
warming to old rhythms.

Old joys, old trusts
cluster around the spine!
Again, from its scaffolding,

all the organs in union.

Members throwing bridges,
anchor lines, drags, a stream of tackle,
an age-old pattern

flesh on rock.

Like the dreaming body
daring leaps the mind can't follow, she
thrusts herself backwards, from ledge to ledge.

Ballet. *Jeté*. Returning on a web.

A Rock near Lutsen

This rock works
silently
against the time
the water takes
from its side.
It allows
my arrival;
the exit
of a beetle
from a crack;
a waterfly
and a rainpool;
a harebell
in a sandskin
of its time.

The Red Horse

In this lake lives the red horse.
Through underwater chambers
he swims featherbreathed past
the hooks of fathers at their windows,
past the hooks of their daughters
who covet his house near the water.
He swims towards the door's blue lintel,
falls
through clouds, cries of gulls.
He spins and spins,
suspending his silver to the sun.

Young Birch

In the lee of the hill,
a stand of young birch,
their own close celebration,
a thousand small flags
fluttering to sun and wind.

I stand very still
to catch their colors.
I hear the small rips
they make in the air.

Irises

painting by Vincent Van Gogh
Metropolitan Museum of Art

Vincent went wild
in the blue iris garden,
compulsively cutting
flowers and blades.
He brought in an armload,
stuffed them in a pitcher
letting them fall
any which way
while he ran for brushes.

They're orchids.
Tongues. Fists soft as felt.
Clitoris thrust up
on a bed of blue silk.
They lust for stimulation,
his own light, quick strokes.

Household Secrets

LIP PRINT AND SNOW SNAKES

A Different Kind of Failure

"...and every attempt
is a wholly new start and a different kind of failure."

*from "East Coker",*T.S. Eliot

Long before the first plate
slides into the water,
there was the first egg,
the first bowl, the slow
accumulation of pots and pans,
the bead of sweat in the philtrum,
the heat in the kitchen,
the meal on the table.

Mabel, Mabel, clear the table
the beginning is ending,
the revolution has begun.
Left to right, stack to suds,
sink to sink, scrub to rinse.
It's always a circle
with me in the middle.
Cups I can handle, flip,
break on the sink.
I try to get the plug
in tight but the sink
leaks like resentment
will leak, has leaked.

Whatever word or music or insight,
withever thing I might have caught
and held to the light is gone
with the gargle in the drainpipe.
I turn to leave the kitchen
and see the glass I missed.
The lipprint
leers at me.

In the Garden

He doesn't show he hears her question. He tugs down the bill of his cap that came free with their seed-order. Lithe-hipped, he walks by her, as if she didn't stand there on the backstep.

When he's half-way to the garden, the head of his shadow falls towards her, a bobbing temptation, close enough to kick. She doesn't give in. She crosses her arms over her breasts, a nervous angel, waiting for his answer.

He starts talking, low, letting the words fall where they will. She can pick them up. Or not.

She takes one step towards him, trembling. The cast of the angel cracks; first a crooked-elbow, and then from the pieces, Big Bertha emerges, hands on her hips, much larger than his. Big Bertha decides he can go to hell.

Like two walls they go about the garden, without talking; he, boring holes and she, ramming the posts in, repairing the fence, to keep neighbors out.

The Poet's Double on the Phone

The telephone rings—it's for the poet.
Who's this? I ask. *The New Yorker?*
You want her latest poem? She's flown
the coop. To escape the list, she said.
Today, shopping: groceries and liquid
plumber. We pour the plumber down,
let it settle as we make supper,
put away groceries, feed the cat and
change the bedding. By that time,
we'll have eaten, the drain will be
unclogged so we can do the washing. What?
Yes, it's a round-the-clock life.
I keep order so she can write.

Lightning struck this morning.
She said I've got a paycheck for a heart,
a wad of guilt in my frontal lobe,
an obsession somewhere between
Teresa of Avila's and Cinderella's.
What we need, she shouted, is more
Virginia Woolf. Who? I asked
and she burst into tears,
wasting more of her writing time.
I mean, if she really wanted to,
she'd just sit down and get at it.
(After we finish the taxes, that is.
We'll get a refund. We want the money.)

You say you pay for poems?
I'm sorry she missed your call.
She mumbled something about warmer parts
as she went out the door
which she didn't bother to close,
wasting fuel. Well, we'll pay for it.
I make sure, one of us always does.

One-Night Stand

And his name shall be called husband,
lover, father. He shall do wonderful
works of world importance. Love,
abundant as the stars in heaven,
shall shine from his eyes.

And though stars fall
husband will never waver.
All things his hands touch will prosper.
His wife, as she walks through the streets,
will be met with deep bows. Their children
will be wise and beautiful, gazelle and fawns,
colts in spring meadows.

Evenings when the household
meets him at the gate, wife and children
step out to kiss the cheek of the provider
from whose hands milk and honey,
honor and blessing never stop flowing—

a one-night stand.

Whatever

We eat.
We know immediately
we shouldn't have eaten.
Our hindsight is shaken.
This is a queer death,
without shedding blood
or staggering. No one
sees us falling.

Whatever happened to us?

Whatever—what a catch-all!
It cracks wide open and our
love falls into the hands
of whatever's rolling on the bottom.

Whatever happened to us.

The wand that waved,
the knock on the door,
the smiling face, the package,
the gift of the apple.

Too late we remember *Gift*
means poison in German.

A Good Place
For a Bar or an Abbey

Asshole houses—
windows stuffed with paper,
bales of straw stacked
against the crawl space,
machinery dumped out in the yard,
piles of it, hoarded,
like money in the bank.

They watch it like the morning
stool to see how much
they've done.

We were scared.
We thought we would have
to stay out there, in a town
in a terrible storm.
We decided to drive on.

All the wildness ended
on the outskirts of town.
The sky opened—

now we can see
by quarter-moonlight and Venus
foxes asleep under field rakes.
Out of the dawn
a flock of snowbirds startles us,
swirls over the windshield,
disappears into the storm

we're leaving behind us.

Joe

April 7, 1951—
February, 1977

There's a coldness about us
as you lie in the casket.
We're a stiff-armed people
shaking hands

to hold off a kiss.

We look at you in the parlor
your face full of bandaids
but you can't fool me:
I see the hole where the bullet

entered your forehead.

There's a bad-mouthed silence.
There's a mewling in the corner.
There's a smile on your face—
you got your boots

out from under our table.

Wife Beater

Sure he beats the wife, dumb cluck,
she married him didn't she, but
he's never once smoked in front of father
and when he was nineteen, he loved her.

He should have left her right away.
Before she had any kids.
He should have left his crummy job,
told the boss, the rotgut stuff

blamed on him
was the work of his pets, hypocrites,
done behind the boss's back.
Then took the train to Miles City—

one double-breasted, pin-striped suit.
Smooth the brim down on the hat
and let the neon-light play up
the moustache—Yeah, he's still got

the job—bought a Chevie. Not as
pretty as a Pontiac but she's better
than sitting on the shacksteps in summer or
freezing your ass off walking in winter.

She Hides Things

Behind the powder she hides her color.
Behind the girdle, a crooked back.
Behind her back, the sharpest knife—
it's not safe to keep it handy.

She can't sleep.
Her husband's feet
stomp through the kitchen
towards the bedroom
and she worries
if her thoughts have been
well-hidden behind her words
or if he's found the knife.

In the darkness she makes up
an alibi for what the right hand
has kept hidden from the left.

The Enormous Pea

*One thing you can do
with an enormous pea
is make light of it.*
s.c.

A pea rolled off my plate,
rolled past my mother's elbow,
rolled to the edge of the table, fell
rolled past her bare foot and having
no other place to go, stopped
at the leg of my father's chair.

A pea, fat and green, silent
as my mother in her chair.

Mother bent to pick it up.
Father moved his chair to give her room
and in replacing his chair and 200 pounds,
he set a leg down, square in the middle
of the little pea's bare foot.

My heart listened for a cry but the pea
was silent. I watched Father lift his chair
and the pea rolled, in a wavering orbit,
out from under.—Whitemouthed pea!
It's a wonder you weren't crushed!

Why didn't Father pick it up?
Why wasn't Mother quicker?
I reach down to pick it up.
See what happens,
when peas roll off their plates?

The pea, fat and green, bites her lip.
Brave as my mother in her chair.

Counting Horses while Driving to Work

Ahead of me
lines of traffic
stalled by snow.
I pass the time
by counting horses
beside the road.
One, two, a set
of three, a group
of four...horses
feeding
at a trough.
The three stand idle.
Two browns
near the barn
shake their manes
free from flakes.

The traffic moves.
Behind me, the horses
shift
into new
positions,
numbers,
compositions
as the snow
falls all day long.

Assault on the Island

(in 8 parts)

1.

I'm bombarded
with pingpong balls
thrown by a screaming mob
wearing masks—
faces of beautiful children

—they're taking
the door with them.
They'll be back,
with more balls.

2.

I want no part
in this pissing and fucking.
I want to use
quiet words.

No one hears you. Often
your lips don't even move.

3.

Do you hear me?

They talk louder
so they can't.

4.

Look, there!
Outside the window.
Someone has thrown
a pair of ears into the grass.

They look very still.

5.

I reach into the sack,
towards one of the last
bulges, one of the last
tricks.

6.

The natives tend time,
9:28s, 11:13s, 2:07s.
I used to recognize them
by the bunch of keys on their belts,
the triplicates stuffed
into pockets, under hats
until I noticed
keys growing on my waist
and had trouble
keeping a hat on my head.

7.

I forget about the ones
who find the threads
in the lesson and pull
them into questions
which reveal design.
How do they survive?

Check the absence lists for clues.
Maybe they come on days
they hate themselves.
Maybe they're deaf
doppelgänger on remote controls.
Look for use of glass shields
and ear plugs left behind
when they board the boat
that leaves this island.

8.

Such a small group in the boat!
They shake their heads
at all the noise
coming from the island's outline.
"Very ugly," one says.
And they all turn
to their circle in the boat
with the wind
and the forward
motion of the sea.

Friends

With friends
like my ovaries
I share a common
reclusive nature:
we like being home.

My doctor calls them lazy.
Their irregularity
is serious
if the breasts drip.

I squirm, knowing mine—
brought up on tea and
dry as crumpets.
My breasts talk around
certain subjects,
would never dream
of dripping
and if they did
would never mention it.

We enjoy
the luxury
of irregularity—
a quiet exhibition:
friends,
just hanging
around together,
staying at home,
not giving a damn
who knows
how lazy we are.

The Sweeper

I feel oldest when I sweep the floor.
My belly bows naturally towards the dust.
Like a bobbing duck's, my arse spreads
as I bend to ease the strain
of stooping on stiff knees.

Every sweep must have its track.
A certain circle is always made
just so around the kitchen.
A pursive reflection on gathered crumbs
is given on who spilled what and when.
Then salt and dustballs, seeds and dirt
are long-stroked; binned together and
slid neatly into a brown paper sack.

New Arrangements

IRISES AND SNAKE

Back to Dakota

Driving home—
to make some connection
between parents and old child
who's given up and now
accepts the state of barrenness
between her parents.

Things haven't changed.
Wild oats weave up to the steps
to ask for a handout.
In the row of blue grainbins
branches of Russian olives
scrape day-long on the tin—

the way my father's sibilance
scraped on the back of my mother's
blue silence—

         The windshield
reflects parts of my body:
my mother's breasts,
my father's wrists and hands.
I move, they move
into different angles,
arrangements
we could call love.

My Father and Mother

They don't fight anymore.
Mornings they listen to the radio
fo the weather and the names
of those who died last night.
After breakfast we women wash up.
He goes out to water the garden.

Irises border it
like an afterthought:
things he threw out in the alley, grew.
They remind me of the old days;
they have a little dried blood
on their tongues.

Cut Iris

After a few days
the tablecloth around the vase
is dotted with purple stains.
The iris stand like men
whose fists have shrunk—
sad snake heads,
dripping vinegar and water.

Night out with Mom

Before you unlock the door
you pause to consider
what you could send
back with me tomorrow:
one thing more,
a jar of cherries?
You look from me to the face
of the brightest star in the sky.
"That's Mama," you confide.

Star, star, grandmother star!
Home of my mother's daydreams,
cherries in the rented farmhouse,
named star in a cluster
of seven at the table,
all made of Mama's own stuff,
cold light and dust.

With all Grandmother's might
I command myself to you.
My arms move

but you've opened the door.
We enter single file,
mother, daughter. Grandmother
shines on,
an armslength
above the roof.

Swimming

Once when I had the pool to myself
I slipped out of my lane and side-stroked,
zigzagged from edge to edge and swam
in wide circles. The water
like a father, held me under my belly and
my spine became as supple as an otter's
as she curves
among the rushes along the shore
or swims straight out to the ocean where

whales
with their gift of perfect spines
swim among their fathomless lanes: leagues-
long and wide. They sing, snort boisterously
as their father's hand holds them
just under their great bellies. They swim
as if they're going on forever.

The Fritz Goes Swimming

for Carolyn Nelson

It's garret-hot. Even the Fritz,
the gray tabby lying in the open window,
is thinking of going swimming.

Eyes half-open, jaw sagging,
she tests the water, blinks,
shivers and falls in.

In a far corner of her eye
you can catch a glimpse of Fritz
in the sea, swimming,
dreamily, to and fro, through
the waves, falling and rising.

A motorcycle roars by the beach.
Even underwater the noise reaches
Fritz's ears. She waves and
comes out, shaking her head,
cat on the beach, cool and smiling.

The Writing Lesson

So I tell them about this root 'naus.'
And to get an idea how old it is, our minds
lift, we sail back to Grecian ports.

Our winter skins explode in hot salt air.
Our ears burn, too, at the sailors'
surly tones. We're quick to step aside

for brusque masters and the teetering loads
on the heads of their slaves. We swagger,
joking how we take the word 'nausea' home.

Ships from those ports have long
dissolved in the sand under sea, still,
shadows of their masts lie over our room.

I stand, listening. New hands
ride the waves from word to word
plunging, pushing on to the next crest;

backs sun-blackened, hands rope-burned,
wind in their throats. I hear them
sending, transferring old messages.

Amulet

The day begins, bare, March.
I roll up the shade and a cardinal
flies out of a tree, upsets
the balance of a stiff branch.
On the ground squirrels' corn
depicts the severity of snow. Then
you enter the room and we
become reflected in the window,
embracing, round as an amulet
held to the morning's scant light.

Night Rain

Night rain falls on the corrugated roof.
In bed, close to the window, we hear it drum
on the eaves, right above our heads,
a tacky, sodden beat smart people escape.
Outside their Volvo guns away
through the downpour, pedal to the floor.

A crazy place for an anchor—our floor.
A curse as sure as a sheet-iron roof.
Or is it a fluke? If we could find a way
to still the rain, deafening out eardrums
with uproarious noise: I mean, escape
down the winding hallways in our heads.

We enter the right side of our heads
and ask for a room on the ground floor
in this lodge, where we've headed to escape
the rain's clamor, a hammer on the roof.
Oh, sweet quiet! A distant horn, not a drum
sounds through a window. Hounds lead the way,

the hunt for the fox, through a mist, away
from the lodge. At a window we watch the heads
of riders swallowed by fog. Hoofs drum
the heath's sod into silence. A creaky floor
behind us—*Herr Ober* announces supper in the roof
garden. We'll eat in our room, our escape.

A common pastime by lovers who escape!
He nods and leads us down the hall, away
from the stairs to the rooms near the roof.
Our feet hurry over Persian rugs. Pegheads
stud the planks in the blond, oak floor.
Herr Ober's heels click like tiny drums.

In our room we light a fire. Like snaredrums
the flames spit and snap a beat to our escape.
We turn to each other, let fall to the floor
our inhibitions. The floor tucks them away.
Warm in bed, under antlers of reddeer heads
we sip on wine, forget the rain and the roof.

Let the humdrum rain bang away.
We've found an escape, nestle our heads
on a ground floor, far from a tinny roof.

The Cricket Frogs

The cricket frogs are out!
Out in the middle of the field,
out of the black, winter ice!

In praise of mud
they make knuckle-cracking noise.
They offer every hour one thousand
pieces of bone and joint.

A red-shawled blackbird
preside over the rite, chants
between his own repeated chimes.

Oh, white day-moon, rejoice!
The back of winter is broken
and a pool of cricket frogs
has just oozed out.

Snake

Poor snake, never to fly
from the underside of leaves
or the bright spot on the rock as
some worms can when transformed.

Instead you write
across the sand on your belly,
the support of your brain and
the length of your tail.

Dark monk! You delight
in keeping your head
properly in place
under your hood.

With no arms or hands
you slough off your skin.
You scare us, we make you
a symbol of life.

Crows

"Sin boldly."
M. Luther

These two crows,
big and lustrous,
peck at the snow on the branch,
a slippery snake
wriggling in their beaks.
For no reason, they let it go.
Their decision gathers power.
Cawing raucously, "Joy! Joy!"
they lift their wings and
dive into the glacial air.

An Arrangement of Wildflowers:
Hyssop and Bergamot

The wildness of hyssop and bergamot
is a feathery lavender, the color of cloth
Corinthian women sold to kings.

The wildness of hyssop and bergamot
is arranged like a fan to arc
the plainness of the kitchen table.

Found in a clump down by the tracks,
these flowers stood in the wind between
diesels, their neck muscles tight

and if they screamed
no one heard
as the trains roared by.

But this arrangement doesn't fit—
standing in a glass, a bog
of tear-and-needle-shaped leaves.

Like fingers, the flowers splay.
They cast a wild crack of light
around this table.

Raking Leaves

for my dad

He decides not to bag the leaves.
He rakes them out of the spindly nets
in the grass. In scoops, flouting town
ordinances, he sends them on
into the wind, barreling down the street.

Now they're flying over the tracks,
out of town. Over the viaduct
the leaves catch an up-blast and
ride it to the river.

A few gingerly
land on the water,
bob on the waves.

The rest swirl on,
towards the Missouri's ring
of blue-and-yellow hills.

He watches them.
The pasty skin of retirement
lighter. All evidence
of disobedience gone
and waltzing on...on...

Evening Walk in October

We drive to a place where
we can walk. On our toes
we go uphill so if the deer
are grazing on the lee
we can sneak closer.

They leap away, the stride
between foreleg and hindleg
marvelously co-ordinated, long
measures of muscled silence
through the weeds
into the woods.

The moon
rises and is held
like the host over the cup.

We head back to the car.
Our shadows dawdle behind us—
children deliberately trying
to lose themselves
in the direction of the deer.

Walking near Dresser, Wisconsin

The farm lay on an arm of the hill—
curled up snug as children will—
I wanted to stay there forever,
to own the oak, and this farmer's house,
the stones stuck in his pasture;
the moss, the moss. From the barn's eaves,
a flock of pigeons, flew up, wheeled.
Light fell through their wings.

A passing car broke the spell.
When I looked again, the birds were gone.
The oak stuck out like a ragged man.
The back of the barn made a good wall.
What carried down the road was housesmoke,
and the melancholy musk of roots.

Carl's Stone

The last time we visited,
Uncle Carl gave me a box of N.D. spuds
and this stone—

bumpy as pitted skin. It smacks
against the fat in the palm.

It must weigh a pound.
It looks like a potato
(and Carl found it in a field.)
It could have been a pestle,
a hammerhead or a tomahawk or a ball
children pitched from hand to hand
as they stood in a circle on the Great Plains
clowning. Razzing anyone
who missed the pitch...

       probably a tight-lipped child,
       Laughter's Shadow, Owl Song,
       Miss Stumbling Block. So intent
       that no one in the circle
       spoil the game,
       she drops the stone.

I can see whoever found it,
running back to the cave, the camp, the barn.

       "Look each one says, out of breath,
       in one language after another.
       For some, not one word left
       nor an echo of the word
       for 'stone,' 'uncle,' 'rock-finder.'

I hold Carl's stone.
My pulse beats like a small heart
under the skin of a drum
held at a distance.
I'm standing on the Plains
alone in the wind and
get caught off guard
by the lightness of my appearance.

THE MINNESOTA VOICES PROJECT

1981

#1 Deborah Keenan, HOUSEHOLD WOUNDS (poems), $3.00

#2 John Minczeski, THE RECONSTRUCTION OF LIGHT (poems), $3.00

The First Annual Competition:

#3 John Solensten, THE HERON DANCER (stories), $5.00

#4 Madelon Sprengnether Gohlke, THE NORMAL HEART (poems), $3.00

#5 Ruth Roston, I LIVE IN THE WATCHMAKERS' TOWN (poems), $3.00

#6 Laurie Taylor, CHANGING THE PAST (poems), $3.00

1982

#7 Alvaro Cardona-Hine, WHEN I WAS A FATHER (a poetic memoir), $4.00

The Second Annual Competition:

#8 Richard Broderick, NIGHT SALE (stories), $5.00

#9 Katherine Carlson, CASUALTIES (stories), $5.00

#10 Sharon Chmielarz, DIFFERENT ARRANGEMENTS (poems), $3.00

#11 Yvette Nelson, WE'LL COME WHEN IT RAINS (poems), $3.00

Copies of any or all of these books may be purchased direct from the publisher, New Rivers Press, Inc., 1602 Selby Avenue, St. Paul, MN 55104 or from your local bookseller.